KHURBN
& OTHER POEMS

Also by Jerome Rothenberg

Poems

White Sun Black Sun   (1960)
The Seven Hells of the Jigoku Zoshi   (1962)
Sightings I–IX   (1964)
The Gorky Poems   (1966)
Between: Poems 1960–1963   (1967)
Conversations   (1968)
Poems 1964–1967   (1968)
Poems for the Game of Silence   (1971)
Poland/1931   (1974)
Gematria 27   (1975)
The Notebooks   (1976)
A Seneca Journal   (1978)
Abulafia's Circles   (1979)
Vienna Blood   (1980)
That Dada Strain   (1983)
New Selected Poems 1970–1985   (1986)

Translations

New Young German Poets   (1959)
Hochhuth's "The Deputy," playing version   (1965)
Enzensberger's "Poems for People Who Don't Read Poems," with Michael
    Hamburger   (1968)
The Book of Hours & Constellations, or Gomringer by Rothenberg   (1968)
The 17 Horse Songs of Frank Mitchell X–XIII   (1970)
15 Flower World Variations   (1984)

Anthologies

Ritual   (1966)
Technicians of the Sacred   (1968, 1985)
Shaking the Pumpkin   (1972, 1986)
America a Prophecy, with George Quasha   (1973)
Revolution of the Word   (1974)
A Big Jewish Book, with Harris Lenowitz and Charles Doria   (1977)
Exiled in the Word, with Harris Lenowitz   (1989)

Recordings

From a Shaman's Notebook   (1968)
Origins & Meanings   (1968)
Horse Songs & Other Soundings   (1975)
6 Horse Songs for 4 Voices   (1978)
Jerome Rothenberg Reads Poland/1931   (1978)

Prose

Pre-Faces & Other Writings   (1981)

JEROME ROTHENBERG

KHURBN
& OTHER POEMS

A NEW DIRECTIONS BOOK

ACKNOWLEDGMENTS
Seven Flag Poems appeared as a separate volume from Arundel Press (Los Angeles, 1989, with etchings by Allan D'Arcangelo) and *Millennium* from Tetrad Press (London, 1988, with illustrations by Ian Tyson). Many of the other poems have appeared in *Sulfur* and in the following magazines and anthologies: *Caliban, Ergo, Fell Swoop, Friendly Local Press, The Green American Tradition, Los Angeles Weekly, New Directions 50* and *52, Paris Exiles, Poésie Internationale Anthologie* (Luxembourg), *The Poet Exposed* (ed. Christopher Felver), *The Poetry Archive Newsletter* (San Diego), *River Styx, Shirim, Temblor, Theater Review* (Binghamton, New York), and *The World.* "Visions of Jesus" was originally published in Jerome Rothen-berg's *New Selected Poems* (New Directions, 1986).

Manufactured in the United States of America
New Directions Books are printed on acid-free paper.
First published clothbound and as New Directions Paperbook 679 in 1989
Published simultaneously in Canada by Penguin Books Canada Limited

Library of Congress Cataloging-in-Publication Data
Rothenberg, Jerome, 1931–
     Khurbn & other poems / Jerome Rothenberg.
       p. cm.
     ISBN 0-8112-1108-8.—ISBN 0-8112-1109-6 (pbk.)
     I. Title. II. Title: Khurbn and other poems.
PS3568.O86K47   1989   89-12224
811'.54—dc20   CIP

New Directions Books are published for James Laughlin
by New Directions Publishing Corporation,
80 Eighth Avenue, New York 10011

CONTENTS

KHURBN

IKONS

for Robert Duncan, comrade [d. 1988] . . .

. . . Now be the angel of my poem.

Khurbn

Since the hidden is bottomless, totality is more invisible than visible.   (Clayton Eshleman)

In 1987 I was a decade, more, past *Poland/1931*. I went to Poland for the first time & to the small town, Ostrow-Mazowiecka, sixty miles northeast of Warsaw, from which my parents had come in 1920. The town was there and the street, Miodowa (meaning "honey"), where my father's parents had a bakery. I hadn't realized that the town was only fifteen miles from Treblinka, but when we went there (as we had to), there was only an empty field & the thousands of large stones that make up the memorial. We were the only ones there except for a group of three people—another family perhaps—who seemed to be picnicking at the side. This was in sharp contrast to the crowds of tourists at Auschwitz (Oswiecim) & to the fullness of the other Poland I had once imagined. The absence of the living seemed to create a vacuum in which the dead—the dibbiks who had died before their time—were free to speak. It wasn't the first time that I thought of poetry as the language of the dead, but never so powerfully as now. Those in my own family had died without a trace—with one exception: an uncle who had gone to the woods with a group of Jewish partisans and who, when he heard that his wife and children were murdered at Treblinka, drank himself blind in a deserted cellar & blew his brains out. That, anyway, was how the story had come back to us, a long time before I had ever heard a word like holocaust. It was a word with which I never felt comfortable: too Christian & too beautiful, too much smacking of a "sacrifice" I didn't & still don't understand. The word with which we spoke of it was the Yiddish-Hebrew word, khurbn (khurban), & it was this word that was with me all the time we stayed in Poland. When I was writing *Poland/1931*, at a great distance from the place, I decided deliberately that that was not to be a poem about the "holocaust." There was a reason for that, I think, as there is now for allowing my uncle's khurbn to speak

3

through me. The poems that I first began to hear at Treblinka are the clearest message I have ever gotten about why I write poetry. They are an answer also to the proposition—by Adorno & others—that poetry cannot or should not be written after Auschwitz. Our search since then has been for the origins of poetry, not only as a willful desire to wipe the slate clean but as a recognition of those other voices & the scraps of poems they left behind them in the mud.

4

IN THE DARK WORD, KHURBN
all their lights went out

their words were silences,
memories
drifting along the horse roads
onto malkiner street

a disaster in the mother's tongue
her words emptied
by speaking

returning to a single word
the child word
spoken, redeyed on
the frozen pond

was how they spoke it,
how I would take it from your voice
& cradle it

that ancient & dark word

those who spoke it in the old days
now held their tongues

1
DOS OYSLEYDIKN (THE EMPTYING)

at honey street in ostrova
where did the honey people go?
empty   empty
miodowa empty
empty bakery & empty road to warsaw
yellow wooden houses & houses plastered up with stucco
the shadow of an empty name still on their doors
shadai & shadow shattering the mother tongue
the mother's tongue but empty
the way the streets are empty where we walk
pushing past crowds of children
old women airing themselves outside the city hall
old farmers riding empty carts down empty roads
who don't dispel but make an emptiness
a taste of empty honey
empty rolls you push your fingers through
empty sorrel soup dribbling from their empty mouths
defining some other poland
lost to us the way the moon
is lost to us
the empty clock tower measuring her light four ways
sorrel in gardens mother of god at roadsides
in the reflection of the empty trains
only the cattle bellow in
like jews the dew-eyed wanderers
still present   still the flies
cover their eyeballs
the trains drive eastward, falling
down a hole (a holocaust) of empty houses
of empty ladders leaning against haystacks no one climbs
empty ostrova & empty ostrolenka
old houses empty in the woods near vyzhkov
dachas the peasants would rent to you
& sleep in stables

the bialo forest spreading to every side
retreating the closer we come to it to claim it
empty oaks & empty fir trees
a man in an empty ditch who reads a book
the way the jews once read
in the cold polish light   the fathers sat there too
the mothers posed at the woods' edge
the road led brightly to treblinka
& other towns   beaches at brok
along the bug
marshes with cattails
cows tied to trees
past which their ghosts walk
their ghosts refuse to walk
tomorrow in empty fields of poland
still cold against their feet
an empty pump black water drips from
will form a hill of ice
the porters will dissolve with burning sticks
they will find a babe's face at the bottom
invisible & frozen imprinted in the rock

2

. . . PASSING CHELMNO ON THE MAIN ROAD DRIVING PAST IT . . .

In May,
along the road to Warsaw,

little ghosts
of Lidice.

A row of peasants
cutting up the earth

on bended
knees.

A man spiffs up
a roadside shrine,

leaving a bunch of
tacky flowers.

Little figures
bathing in the Warta.

Little thought
to what was there.

3

HIDDEN IN WOODS   BAGGED
like an Indian

a cry (darkest in
the pauses)

cannot be heard   But inward
he discerns it

what his life had been
& several   trusting in him

(children

or the dead) life's burden
I cannot escape it any longer

in a vodka sleep (the cry
cutting still deeper

into his bones)   Bright spots
a zohar of possibilities

a father's cry

(oh mother hold me) how I have lost
my tongue

my hand chewed down
to the bone   must bellow

like a heifer
& crawling through their blood

my children severed from me
(their souls

stuck in my mouth   teeth
frozen

the room turns to ice

in moonlight

it flies through the woods

a cry   a spirit
his death turns loose

with no roots
runs deeper   the cry you can hear

is no cry

4
DOS GESHRAY (THE SCREAM)

Erd, zolst nit tsudekn mayn blut
un zol nit kayn ort zayn far mayn geshray
(Job 16:18)

"practice your scream" I said
(why did I say it?)
because it was his scream & wasn't my own
it hovered between us   bright
to our senses always bright it held
the center place
then somebody else came up & stared
deep in his eyes there found a memory
of horses galloping faster the wheels dyed red
behind them   the poles had reserved
a feast day but the jew
locked in his closet screamed
into his vest a scream
that had no sound therefore
spiraled around the world
so wild that it shattered stones
it made the shoes piled in the doorway
scatter their nails   things testify
—the law declares it—
shoes & those dearer objects
like hair & teeth do
by their presence
I cannot say that they share the pain
or show it not even the photos
in which the expressions of the dead shine forth
the crutches by their mass the prosthetic limbs by theirs
bear witness the eyeglasses bear witness
the suitcases the children's shoes the german tourists
in the stage set oshvientsim had become
the letters over its gates still glowing

11

still writ large
ARBEIT MACHT FREI
& to the side   HOTEL
and GASTRONOMIC BAR
the spirit of the place dissolving
indifferent to his presence
there with the other ghosts
the uncle   grieving
his eyelids turning brown an eye
protruding from his rump
this man whose body
is a crab's
his gut turned outward
the pink flesh of his children
hanging from him
that his knees slide up against
there is no holocaust
for these   but khurbn only
the word still spoken by the dead
who say   my khurbn
& my children's khurbn
it is the only word that the poem allows
because it is their own
the word as prelude to the scream
it enters
through the asshole
circles along the gut
into the throat
& breaks out
in a cry   a scream
it is his scream that shakes me
weeping   in oshvientsim
& that allows the poem to come

5
DIBBUKIM (DIBBIKS)

spirits of the dead   lights
flickering (he said) their ruakh
will never leave the earth
instead they crowd the forests the fields
around the privies the hapless spirits
wait millions of souls
turned into ghosts at once
the air is full of them
they are standing each one beside a tree
under its shadows or the moon's
but they cast no shadows of their own
this moment & the next they are pretending
to be rocks   but who is fooled
who is fooled here   by the dead   the jews
the gypsies   the leadeyed polish patriot
living beings reduced to symbols
of what it had been to be alive
"o do not touch them" the mother cries
fitful, as almost in a dream
she draws the child's hand to her heart
in terror   but the innocent dead
grow furious they break down doors
drop slime onto your tables
they tear their tongues out by the roots
& smear your lamps your children's lips
with blood a hole drilled in the wall
will not deter them
from stolen homes stone architectures
they hate they are the convoys of the dead
the ghostly drivers still searching
the roads to malkin   ghost carts overturned
ghost autos in blue ditches
if only our eyes were wild enough
to see them our hearts to know their terror

the terror of the man who walks alone
their victim whose house whose skin
they crawl in   incubus & succubus
a dibbik leaping from a cow to lodge inside
his throat   clusters of jews
who swarm here mothers without hair
blackbearded fathers
they lap up fire   water   slime
entangle the hairs of brides
or mourn their clothing hovering
over a field of rags   half-rotted shoes
& tablecloths   old thermos bottles   rings
lost tribes in empty synagogues
at night their voices
carrying across the fields
to rot your kasha your barley
stricken beneath their acid rains
no holocaust because no sacrifice
no sacrifice to give the lie
of meaning   & no meaning   after auschwitz
there is only poetry   no hope
no other language left to heal
no language   & no faces
because no faces left   no names
no sudden recognitions on the street
only the dead still swarming   only khurbn
a dead man in a rabbi's clothes
who squats   outside the mortuary house
who guards their privies who is called
master of shit   an old alarm clock
hung around his neck   who holds
a wreath of leaves under his nose
from eden   "to drive out
"the stinking odor of this world"

6

THE OTHER SECRET IN THE TRAIL OF MONEY
& all true all true the poet's vision
proven in the scraps. Bank notes & zlotys strewn
over the field. Papers buried. Testaments
to death & to the acquisitive nature of the guards
its passage from hand to hand, to make a picnic
in the Jewish State. Imagine.
That he is again in the field leading to the showers & that the
field is strewn with money. Those who are dead have left it, &
the living bend to pick it up. The rhythms of Gold's orchestra
drift past him, as in the woods sometimes the squeals of chil-
dren & women or the deeper bellows of the men. He bends to
lift a coin or to remove a bag of chocolates & raisins from a
dead girl's coat. Butter. Cheese. White rolls. Roast chicken.
Cognac. Cream. Sardines. "More sugar & tea than in the whole
Warsaw ghetto." The Jewish workers & their guards feast in
the woods. A child is with them—turns her mouth to you—
that by gematria becomes a hole.

7
DER GILGUL (THE POSSESSED)

1

he picks a coin up
from the ground

it burns his hand
like ashes it is red

& marks him as it marks
the others   hidden

he is hidden in the forest
in a world of nails

his dibbik fills him

2

Each night another one would hang himself. Airless boxcars.
Kaddish. "What will they do with us?" The brown & black
spots on their bellies. So many clothes. The field was littered.
Ten thousand corpses in one place. Arranged in layers. I am
moving down the field from right to left—reversing myself at
every step. The ground approaches. Money. And still his great-
est fear was that he would lose his shoes.

3

earth, growing fat with
the slime of corpses   green & pink

that ooze like treacle, turn
into a kind of tallow

that are black
at evening   that absorb

all light

8
NOKH AUSHVITS (AFTER AUSCHWITZ)

the poem is ugly & they make it uglier
wherein the power resides
that duncan did—or didn't—understand
when listening that evening to the other poet read
he said   "that was pure ugliness"   & oh it was
it was   & it made my heart skip a beat
because the poem wouldn't allow it   no
not a moment's grace nor beauty to obstruct
whatever the age demanded   or the poem
shit poured on wall & floor
sex shredded   genitals torn loose by dog claws
& the ugliness that you were to suffer
later   that they had suffered
not as dante dreamed it but in the funnel
they ran through & that the others called
the road to heaven   little hills & holes now
& beneath   upon   among them
broken mirrors kettles pans enameled teapots
the braided candlesticks of sabbath
prayershawl scraps & scraps of bodies   bones
his child's   he said   leaping
into the mud the pool of bones
& slime   the frail limbs separating
each time he pulls at one   the mystery of body
not a mystery   bodies naked   then bodies
boned & rotten   how he must fight
his rage for beauty must make a poem
so ugly it can drive out the other voices
like artaud's squawk the poem addressed
to ugliness   must resist
even the artistry of death   a stage set
at treblinka   ticket windows   a large clock
the signs that read: change for bialystok
but the man cries who has seen

18

the piles of clothing   jews
it is not good it is your own sad meat
that hangs here   poor & bagged   like animals
the blood coagulated into a jell
an armpit through which a ventricle has burst
& left him dangling screaming
a raw prong stuck through his tongue
another through his scrotal sac   he sees
a mouth   a hole   a red hole
the scarlet remnants of the children's flesh
their eyes like frozen baby scallops
so succulent that the blond ukrainian guard
sulking beneath his parasol leaps up
& sucks them inward past his iron teeth
& down his gullet, shitting
globules of fat & shit
that trickle down the pit in which the victim—
the girl without a tongue—stares up
& reads her final heartbreak

9

THOSE WHO ARE BEAUTIFUL & THOSE WHO
ARE NOT
change places   to relive
a death by excrement

victims thrown into the pit & drowning
in their ordure
suffocating in the body's dross

this is extremity

these images of shit, too raw
for feeling,
that drips onto their faces

women squatting on long planks
to shit "like birds
perched on a telegraph wire"

who daub each other

have no language for the horror
left to speak, the stink
has so much caked their throats,

they who would live with shit
& scrape it
from drinking cups

this is extremity   this place

is where desire ends
where the warm flux inside the corpse
changes to stone

THE DOMAIN OF THE TOTAL CLOSES AROUND
    THEM   for there is even
totality here   a parody of telos   of completion
in the monstrous mind of the masters   those who give them-
    selves authority
over the rest of life   who dole out life & death   propor-
    tioned
to their own appetites as artists   they forge a world   a
    shadow image of our own
& are the artists of the new hell   the angels of the possible
    the vision
passed from them down to the present   of what art can do
    what constructs of the mind
are thinkable   when power assists their hands   in the de-
    lusion of the absolute
"a universe of death"   where hell's thrust upward toward
    the surface   becomes the vital fact
a row of chimneys spewing flames into the night smoke burst-
    ing from holes & ditches   swirling swaying coiling above
    their heads
"the sparks & cinders blinded us" (the scroll reads) "through
    the screened fence of the second crematory we could see
    figures with pitchforks moving against the background of
    flames
"turning the corpses in the pits so densely packed it seemed
    that death had welded them together"
the faces of the uncovered dead twist in the flames that touch
    them
seem to come back to life   exuding lymph & fat
that oozes from them   eyes exploding   like the belly
of the pregnant woman   bursting open   now expels
its fetus   that goes up in flames

. . . .

2

but at the camp's outer edge new buildings rise a paradise of
    painted doors
a lane of flowers a pond in which a stone frog sits a little
    wooden bench set at the brink with pastoral animals brave
    shepherds
it is this other camp that haunts him now that haunts *me* this
    with its sculpted images of jews
the faces sharp & bright that show no trace of suffering but
    eyes aflame turn toward their future
& sing bravely the song of work & death that the masters had
    enjoined that gold had written for them
ecstatic jews in wood & always bowing pointing to the jewish
    state that lies within
yours is the world of art writ large art joined to life until the
    boundaries split apart
the measure struck by gold's orchestra a sound so sweet that
    even the masters swayed to it
so did the jews bring tears to eyes already dark with smoke so
    would the jews bring tears again
whom later in the market place in krakow we would see anew
their noble wooden faces & marbled eyes fulfilling the dream
    of life
the gold jews & the jews of death exchanging places
they for whom money lies beneath the field   under the bar-
    racks floor   & buys them time
the corpses melt   the plaza jews trade garbage in the square
the hapless jews slowly fall backwards & are buried in the
    ditch
the band is in white dinner jackets trimmed in blue with
    staves on the lapels & trousers blue stripes along the seams
the court jews live in private rooms & give their children edu-
    cations waiting
for the night to come again the cabaret to start its doleful
    music where bad art
to bad art's joined the heart grows murky weeps at its own
    losses but drones on

.   .   .   .   .   .

22

3

THE SONG

"the sound of workers'
"feet   marching
"faces in ice, dark faces

"battalions on their way
"to work   the faithful
"& the brave   (they say)

"this brings us here,
"treblinka-bound, the end
"a breath away & carried

"in the master's voice
"it is the thunder, is the way
"he looks or we look

"bunched in columns, docile
"docile, must obey or die
"(they say) we do not want

"to leave you   destiny
"is anywhere we turn
"it casts an eye on us,

"will find us waiting here
"faces in ice, battalions
"marching   one final day

. . . . . .

4

the assignators even here   breathing thru the lungs of the
ill-fated Max Bielas   handsome man who had a harem
of little jewish boys & dressed them to the delight of
all who visited in perfect white blouses & dark blue hosen
over tummies & butts so round & firm he trembled   yawned
sent them to tend the flock of geese a row of pretty boys
dressed up like princes   & had a fabled dream house
built for them   of roughhewn logs   lace curtains   in
      which
they slept they sang they waited in the afternoons
for uncle Max to come to them   sweet
german daddy bringing little cakes & *schlag* or letters
from the folks out east   they were his dwarfs & he
their gentle snow white swooning when they pressed around
      him
when he touched a tiny hand or let his thumb slide down
the young back proffered to him   redfaced   eager   to
      become a victim to his victim
the bright pornography of death implicit in each breath
each word the mind imagines   it is desire that compels him
directs the flow the force engulfing him & them
all in the name of love that has delivered many to this place
as hate has   the goods of the intellect reduced
& bounded   by the craving self   protected from the world
where the mind & the body go astray   theirs is no simple
      wish
for death or order but toward that greater ugliness
debasement breeds   this that de sade foretold   that the
      young mind of isidore ducasse
tracked to his own destruction   so sweet it is so sickening
we pull away from it although it holds us (we who were young
      enough were old enough to be its victims)
it makes us gag & scream here where we listen to the other
      voices
of those who were abandoned those whom desire fondled
until in the aftermath of his own death his cravings spent the
      other killers entered

24

restored them to the silent world where no love is
where they were returned to light   & dust   cut loose   in
        flesh's color
into the house of pain

.   .   .   .

5
the grandfather who would have carried god with him
into the pit   would he have cursed as I will for him?

or for that uncle who died, surely, with a malediction on his
      tongue
screamed it until the tongue dissolved the bullet achieved its
     mark bit deeper

into a world of fact (alas) the mind that cries cried out
"the god is real he whom the dead bear with them

"who bear witness to the death of metaphor & cry:
"do not forget us! help us! think of us!"

he is a man called yoshka is a name we share that grandfather
     & I
name that the jews called jesus that they screamed out of the
     slime

the world is god's then   & its ugliness   follows from his
therefore they love the female form   the boundaries

no one can know or guess but sometimes discern it in
the mother   she like an absent god   stripped into naked-
     ness

along the fivefold stages of her way the windows tight shut
     around her
brightly painted the fixed hands of the giant clock still stuck
     at three

their spirits still wandering who will never rest
babes thrown hapless to the flames the eyes & tongues of the
    old men torn out

o god of caves (the stricken fathers cry) if you are light
then there can be no metaphor

11
DI MAGILAS FUN AUSHVITS
(THE SCROLLS OF AUSCHWITZ)

He had vanished & reappeared in a room no bigger than a giant's hand. Asleep in it. His arms & legs were rusted, his eyes swam in his head like mercury. He was twice forgotten. A stranger to his memory of who he was.

When a man moves up & down across the field, the earth moves with him. The condition is described as double thunder—repeated by the ones called souls, the hopeless dead. It is most likely they who move, the rest is an illusion. The stranger in the giant's hand knows who they are.

Dibbik legions perch on trees. The trees die. Then the sun gives birth to basilisks. A basilisk gives birth to what the rock conceals. True life is punctuated. It eats through time & breeds out of the sun. The sexual is its other head worn on its other body. It is your body too & tries to run from you. You brush against it with your hand.

Once the dibbik was a singular occurrence. It is now repeated many million times as the result of so much early death. Into whom do the dead souls enter? Each one contains a dibbik, or some of them contain a world of dibbiks. Hijikata writes: "To make the gestures of the dead, to die again, to make the dead enact their deaths again, this is what I want to feel. The dead are my teachers & live inside me."

A hand is like a hole. I know it & he knows it too. Was he there? No. No more than I was. But the dead have found him & eaten through his skin. He feels them in the morning when he shits: a gnawing pain beneath his heart. The dead who were burnt alive are still the hopeless dead. Thus the ceremony-of-burning is a lie. And thus the holocaust.

In the dream 3000 naked women cry in pain. It is impossible to count them but he does. Their bodies will be used for kindling, their blood for fuel. No one will cry or turn away, but sometimes the wind will force a tear out of his eye, & his tongue & teeth will follow, flying from his mouth. "Ah," the young girl will say, her legs twisted behind her back. "The tear of a live Jew will go with me to my death."

The room he looked into now was still smaller. It looked like a regular shower room with all the accoutrements of a public bathhouse. The walls of the room were covered with small, white tiles. It was very fine, clean work. The floors were covered with orange terra cotta tiles. Nickle-plated metal faucets were set into the ceiling.

It was in Poland that I realized I was haunted. Yes. "A dibbik is in me. A dibbik is in me." It is the condition of our lives for forty years now. Hijikata confirms it for us, that poetry is the speech of ghosts. The shamans in your books confirm it. In *my* books I meant to say. And didn't.

[Gradowski's Testament] A black & white world, sky & earth. The court of angry shadows. These. Broken into. The open mouth of earth prepared to swallow us alive. The last. His world a tinted film. A bent black mass. Black shadows. Swallowed up in railroad cars. Gradowski's testament. Along the white road. Thousands crawling on all fours. Two women at the roadside, crying. People shrunk to half their size. A finger moves across her throat. "Take interest in this document. Keep looking. You will find still more."

From now on we will bury everything in the earth.

12
DER VIDERSHTAND (THE RESISTANCE)

began with this in olson's words it was
the pre/face   so much fat for soap
superphosphate for soil   fillings & shoes for sale
such fragmentation delivered by whatever means
the scrolls of auschwitz buried   now brought to light
again   the words of zalman lowenthal of poland
who had been dragged into the woods who saw
"the damned plays of liquidation"—incredible (he wrote)
the ocean seeping across the empty field
inside his head   how like a sump   how grungy
the world reduced to yellow flesh & mud
the man in black whose hands are in black gloves
has killed them   the red one
still standing at the gates of warsaw
waits   & the other   at the gates of paris   holds
the dark rule now past the 8th month 1944
a game of shootings hangings gassings burnings
written down   between the walls of the black building
from the time he searched for reasons
for his suffering & wrote
about himself "what happened to that jew?"
or the blond girl now a dibbik asked the question
"mister jew what will they do with us?"
& someone—was it him?—said "garbage"
the resistance beginning with the writing down
that the time & mud have faded
the moon adrift in elul   shining
on a certain man concerned
with history who took the trouble
to assemble pictures   facts   reports
to shield them with his body
"this house" wrote olson "where his life is
"where he dwells against the enemy   the beast"
but sees it crumble sees *them* crumble

all around him   this sparagmos
where the flesh turned yellow from the gas
the fire burst it & the fetus
erupted through the mother's skin
a babe's head that the hair is torn from
& brunner the s.s. survivor used the same word "garbage"
in 1987   thus was the epic verified
& brought into our time   the poem
began with it & followed the movement
of the dead man's hand   as if each written word
had such a hand behind it
that brought the letters & the pain together
written with his blood (the scroll says) in the light
of human bodies burning   but what is interesting
here (he writes) is the psychology of man
who refuses to accept
evil thoughts   no matter how clearly he sees
he speaks   for this is not
the whole truth   the truth as it really exists
is immeasurably more tragic & terrible.   In the notebook
    dig to search
it is by chance that this
is buried   by chance that it comes to light
the poetry is there too
it is in the scraps of language
by which the century is read to us the streets the dogs
the faces fading out the eyes receding
they are the dead & want so much to speak
that all the writing in the world will not contain them
but the dead voice crying in the money field
declares it   makes its resistance still
he says   I want to tell you
what my name is   my name is buried
in the ashes   my name
is not a name

13

WHAT MAKES HIM KNEEL DOWN IN THE MUD
kneel down in the money field, to lift up
this wet shining coin

as later he would draw
chocolates & raisins from the young girl's
coat   so deep in mud

the woods do lie, the frost
does cover an old hut
the winds do seem to push the moon

along   or is it the clouds
first moving   or the blood
on everything that he ever loved

& prays now that it soon be ended:
finis moon & finis little world
below the moon

[pause]

FISHL'S SONG

I have no more to live for
—the dead man says—
I leave you with a curse, damned others

& may my voice be true to it
who know no kindly light
but in my death have altered

into a wolf
whose mouth is raw with blood
a ring of blood

covering my beard & throat:
a number larger than the moon
searing my chest

conflated,
still,
opens to let the spirit out

14
DI TOYTE KLOLES (THE MALEDICTIONS)

Let the dead man call out in you because he is a dead man
Let him look at your hands in the light that filters through the
    table where he sits
Let him tell you what he thinks & let your throat gag on his
    voice
Let his words be the poem & the poem be what you wouldn't
    say yourself
Let him say that every man is a murderer & that he is a mur-
    derer like all the rest
Let him say that he would like to beat & kill beat & kill let him
    say that it is nothing nothing nothing
That he is living in a wilderness (let him say it) but that there
    are no woods or trees
That whatever houses there were are gone or if the houses are
    there he cannot enter them or see them
That he cannot see the children that he knows were there that
    he doesn't know if his own children were there too
That he seeks out the children of his enemy & would like to
    kill them
Let those who sit around you hear nothing of what he says let
    them hear everything of what you tell them
Let a great pain come up into your legs (feel it moving like the
    earth moving beneath you)
Let the earth drop away inside your belly falling falling until
    you're left in space
Let his scream follow you across the millennia back to your
    table
Let a worm the size of a small coin come out of the table where
    you're sitting
Let it be covered with the red mucus falling from his nose (but
    only you will see it)
Let the holes in his body drop open let his excretions pour out
    across the room

Let it flood the bottoms of the women's cages let it drip through the cracks into the faces of the women down below

Let him scream in a language you cannot understand let the word "khurbn" come at the end of every phrase

Let a picture begin to form with every scream

Let the screams tell you that the world was formed in darkness that it ends in darkness

Let the screams take you into a room with small white tiles

Let the tiles vanish beneath the press of bodies let vomit & shit be everywhere let semen & menstrual blood run down his arms

Let his screams describe a body (a body is like a stone a body rests on another body & weighs it down a body crushes the skull that lies beneath it a body has arms & reaches for the sky a body has eyes & knows terror in the darkness a body burning gives off heat & light)

Let 10,000 bodies be gathered in one place until they vanish let the earth & sky vanish with them & then return

Let an empty field fill up with coins & let the living bend to pick them up

Let everything have its price let there be a price for death & a price for life so that everything can be accounted

Let them account the value of a body (a soul has no account) & let the living refuse the living unless a price is paid

Let betrayal take the place of love & let disgust be put ahead of beauty

Let she who is most beautiful be brought down to her knees let those who hold together out of love be murdered

Let the dead cry for the destruction of the living until there is no more death & no more life

Let a ghost in the field put out the light of the sun (I have no arms he cries

My face & half my body have vanished & am I still alive?

But the movement of my soul through space & time brings me inside you

The immeasurable part of a language is what we speak he says who am I? dayn mamas bruder farshvunden in dem khurbn

un muz in mayn eygenem loshn redn loz mikh es redn
durkh dir dos vort khurbn
Mayne oygen zaynen blind fun mayn khurbn ikh bin yetst a
peyger) a corpse to which the light will not return forever
for whom the light is lost
Let the light be lost & the voices cry forever in the dark & let
them know no joy in it
Let murders multiply & tortures let fields rot & forests shrink
let children dig up bones under the market square
Let fools wield power let saints & martyrs root up money in a
field of blood
Let madness be the highest virtue let rage choke all who will
not rage
Let children murder children let bombs rain down let houses
fall
Let ghosts & dibbiks overwhelm the living
Let the invisible overwhelm the visible until nothing more is
seen or heard

15

PERORATION FOR A LOST TOWN

[May 1988]: "On this road thou camest . . ."

1

what will I tell you sweet town?
that the sickness is still in you
that the dead continue to die
there is no end to the dying?
for this the departed would have had an answer:
a wedding in a graveyard
for you sweet town
they would have spoken they who are no longer among us
& would have shown forth in their splendor
would have danced pellmell
over your stones sweet town
the living & the dead together   feathers
would have blown like feathers
from their fingers   no   like gold   like roses
like every corny proposition
fathers or uncles ever gave us   they gave us
to call your image back to life
sweet town their voices twittering
like bats over your little houses
is this the sound then that the breath makes
in its final gasp that the dead make
having lived a whole life under water
now coming up for air, to find themselves
in poland in the empty field
bathers who had their bodies torn apart
& ran from you   their long guts
hanging, searching the forgotten woods
for houses & the consolation
that death brings   children in a circle
dancing   without tongues   the meadow that had once
        stood open

shut in remembrance now sweet town
the screams of the cousins carried by the wind
lost in the gentile cities
in the old men's dreams of you
each night sweet town who rise up from their beds
like children   bellowing   their words
stuck in their beards like honey
who drift up brok street past the russian church
the doctor's house beside it heavy
& whitebricked in the dream   who glide above
napoleon square o little orchards little park
where lovers once walked with lovers   children
still capture fishes in thy little pond
its surfaces still green with algae
o sounds of church bells—bimbom—through the frozen air
that call forth death o death o pale photographer
o photos of the sweet town rubbed with blood
o of its streets the photographs its vanished folk
o wanderers who wandered o bodies of the distant dead who
     stayed
o faces o dimming images lost smiles o girls embracing girls
in deathless photographs   o life receding
into images of life   you beautiful & pure   sweet town
I summon & I summon thee to answer

I have come here looking for the bone of my grandfather (I said). Daylight had intervened. The town was no more empty as we walked its length. Then the old man spat—gently—through his beard. I have come here looking for the bone of my son. (Had someone reported a breath of life under his houses—a movement within the soil like worms & caterpillars?) Tell the Poles that they should come to me. I am a baker & a child. I have no one to take me from this darkness.

Then he asked— or was it I who asked or asked *for* him?—were there once Jews here? Yes, they told us, yes they were sure there were, though there was no one here who could remember. What was a Jew like? they asked. (The eye torn from its socket hung against his cheek.) Did he have hair like this? they asked. How did he talk—or did he? Was a Jew tall or short? In what ways did he celebrate the Lord's day? (A rancid smell of scorched flesh choked us.) Is it true that Jews come sometimes in the night & spoil the cows' milk? Some of us have seen them in the mead- ows—beyond the pond. Long gowns they wear & have no faces. Their women have sharppointed breasts with long black hairs around the nipples. At night they weep. (Heads forced in the bowls until their faces ran with excrement.) No one is certain still if they exist. (Plants frozen at the bottom of a lake, its surface covered by thick ice.)

They spoke & paused. Spoke & paused again. If there was a history they couldn't find it—or a map. The cemetery they knew was gone, the dead dispersed. (On summer days the children digging in the marketplace might come across a bone.) And the shops? we asked. The stalls? The honey people? Vanished, vanished in the earth, they said. The red names & the flower names. The pink names. (There was a people once, they said, we called the old believ- ers. A people with black beards & eyes like shriveled raisins. Out of the earth they came & lived among us. When they walked their bodies bent like yours & scraped the ground. They had six fingers on each hand. Their old men had the touch of women when we rubbed against them. One day they

dug a hole and went back into the earth. They live there to
this day.)

The village pump you spoke about still stands back
of the city hall (they told us). The rest was all a dream.

3

[by gematria]

a wheel
dyed red

an apparition

set apart

out of the furnace

Ostrow-Mazowiecka
Poland/1988

Ikons

GOLEM & GODDESS

into the dark of Prague
the golem walks
backwards in the familiar stride
empty of longing
a madman takes   o Loew Loew
in your chair I sat
the shadows in your books
so heavy
hurt my eyes & brought
memories of the children
changing to skeletons
you my old rabbi couldn't
bring to life again
though with your stones I spoke
& heard
old voices through old cities
the victims of the century
that the century will bring together
will offer their own flesh to the hill
somewhere beyond the city
the goddess once built with
the bones of dogs & children
a thousand cities spring from
over europe   & the goddess
still waits above the moldau
the daughter of the morning star
who feeds her son the moon
with children's blood

THE IKON (1)

a female jesus
bearded
& hanging from the cross
looks down on us
teeth biting through her beard
her breasts   pushed high
& popping from the peasant blouse
that make the man who watches feel
deeply & warmly
a rush of sappy propositions
the swirl of fish over his thighs
like wet vanilla
the mothers will lick from him
will tell him stories of
the girl who hated men
whom her own father
hammered to the cross
is now the god
her words transform her into
"grow" she whispers
to the hairs under her skin
that flutter out like worms
& wiggling
bending
will form the godbeard down her cheeks
the little mothers
squeezing cold knives between their thighs
anointing her
"sweet sister misery"
he who is jesus in her flesh
whose mustache on her lip
is heavy   now becomes her
their fingers hammered to the cross
flop down
the male cock issues forth

but hidden   rises up her belly
its swollen thrust between
the breasts of holy misery queen jesus
imagined as a man   whose woman-
part has swallowed
what her nailed hands cannot
touch   "my god"
she calls it
"noli me tangere" the cock says
the clock inside her head
against her tongue
now sees it disappear & rise again
the bed that opens for her now
becomes a lake
an island where three virgins sit
in red   behind a glass
a window in a town
behind the eyes of strangers
watching   stirring
the thick milk of strangers
that issues from between her legs
a dream   a movie
her body's triumph as his own
until she dreams herself
into far cities
her body strung between red lights
a female lamb   she is
my holy lady misery
I reach to in her dream
whose substance
is her beard a tuft of hair around
her wet mouth
where the shaman crosses
a blood river
tufts of hair are floating in
queen jesus   I have become
thy singer minstrel
thy young bard who lifts thee

from thy cross
astonished at
the weight of thee   a doll
become an ikon
aching
throbbing dumbly
brushes the dead light that breaks around us

THE IKON (2)

this morning in a dream   the saint
the bearded lady pulls herself
from sleep   she stares
into the empty mirror
rinses her eyes with rain
kneels down
before the other ikons
who watch her where she paints
her white face whiter
the bearded lady
she in white who straddles
the threshold of the sad abyss
called church   nobody sees
or hears her
but the cries of witches
fill her mind   the noise
of women's hair blown by a wind
who take her out of town, her body
wrapped in a snakeskin
fish smeared on her flesh
& gobs of tar
my saint my golden girl
she squawks & bellows
"nobody sees or hears me
"in bogs of bukovina
"bare homeland where our mothers virgins
"in sleep cry out
"where all women are named mary
"in the gentile tongue
"& wait with golden lamps in starlight
"who lead me down the road to abraham's
"into some drippy jordan where we dip
"our thighs where someone shoves a cuckoo
"down my mouth the neighbors hear
"& dream of nightingales

"they stream onto the roads
"to seek for me
"to stuff my body into velvet
"furs & gabardines against my sex
"my double beard
"who trudge along the distant highways
"where the sick behind their dying eyes
"reach out   the children of the poor
"climb fences   ancient women
"running without shawls
"old men standing capless
"boys who hurt us
"who watch in silence without belts
"& sing to me
" 'o you our babe
" 'of bucharest
" 'who shine
" 'like both the sun & moon
" 'o christ in furs
" 'you sharp & foxy
" 'lady admiral
" 'who strut for us
" 'now & forever
" 'o you our bearded ikon
" 'white & cuddled
" 'into love

THREE FOR THE SUN AS GODDESS

1

old hannah   mother sun
living a hard life
      seen her
some fine evening
running   awaking
with the dew

2

made her a bed of
roses   poppy flowers
for sheets
daughter of old mother sun
would sleep on
with the morning star

3

the daughter of the sun
is opening
a gate   she wears
gloves made of stars,
plants roses in
a silver garden
the sons of god walk by & sprinkle
gold like dew

SONGS FOR MIDSUMMER

1

what is shining, shimmering
on sweet john's night
               (sweet night)?
sweet ferns are flowering
                      (lightly lightly)
sweet golden flowers

2

a field of flowers
I would wade through
               (lightly lightly)
        on sweet john's night
my feet in velvet shoes
my shoes filld up with
golden flowers

3

beat your copper drum
               (sweet john)
& light the fires
the sweet children of sweet john
will come to
            singing
        lightly lightly
on sweet john's night

4

all flowers come to blossoms
                              (lightly lightly)
only sweet ferns do not
except on sweet john's night
                              (sweet night)
in sprays of golden mist

5

a golden chain I drew
out of a silver oak
& drew a man's thoughts through me
                    singing
          lightly lightly
on sweet john's night

The two preceding series of poems are translations from Latvian folk poetry by Jerome Rothenberg and Astride Ivaska.

ANOTHER IKON
Mexico 1984

the doll is god here,
eyeless, he is called
the-little-blind-boy
—plump cheeks, frilly smock
over his thighs—
he rubs himself,
the deep wood
of the cross tightens
his flesh,
o cieguecito,
throne set on cushions,
feet into tiny shoes
with snaps

ALTAR PIECES / 1986

1

jesus at a wedding
waits for us

monkeys with chains around their legs
surround him

dishes of squabs
on tables

the strangers come to wash his feet,
tra la they sing

a boy perched at a window
blows a trumpet

cherries & pears along the floor,
a single fly

2

a man called john,
much like the others

stands barefoot near a lake
with swans & boats

I turn away from him
& wait

another year inside my head
another cycle

then see him, crying
from his cauldron

mad turks surround him,
warts on their noses

pouring water on his head

3/ A VISION OF THE GODDESS, AFTER CRANACH

sage & holy,
she is sharpening a long stick

while on a swing
a babe sails by

the sky fills up with
warriors on goats & boars

a sleeping dog
two quail

a dish of fruit
a castled landscape

4

the priest's hand underneath
the bishop's robe

against the rump, the flesh
envelops him & hides

whatever floats around the dancing
twitching jesus

54

on his altar: heads & hands
tacked onto space

a head propped on a pedestal
a head in midair

separated from the crown,
the spear, the rattling dice

a hand holding a switch
a hand that points

under the dancer's feet
a robe in flames

BELGRADE APOCALYPSE

the animals over our heads
cry out   their bodies
filled with eyes
across the room where christ
his crown a triangle
keeps track of wine & rakia
the dancers bring him
in the small side-chapel
blackened by candlesmoke
the ikons become black masses
a black ceiling
overhead   red sun
outside a swarm of
screaming crows
over the trollies

DEAD BODIES

1

they pretend light
& fall, headlong
into a paper forest

where they awake
forgetting, dreaming
a distended passage

with roots that spread & tear,
seize the wetness
& grow dead from it:

how right to cut our way
out of your shrunken thoughts
into a paper forest

2

the dead,
when we speak to them,
curse
the living

their only words to us
sound badly,
smell
of when they died,

poor lights
that flicker,
barely,
night & day

3

if a hand slides
over your mouth—better
to forget it

& better that the stars
be gathered overhead,
that they exist in space

untouchable,
like god,
or like a thought

your mind has yet to think,
tranquil at last,
the solitary distance of a star

4

the blue face at the window
is a mask, a dog's face
the annunciation of a year of deaths

like the time when we all will die
friends & lovers
we will assume the voice of poetry

as it issues from the dead

5

who vanishes
into time
remains there,

captured child,
despairing
mother's face:

"they will never return
"to grace us
"they will fly to the sky:

"just look at them
"& ponder,
"by what ways your own ways go

6

as lonely
as a dog's soul
in the forest

shining,
open-eyed, like stars
& diamonds

crying in the leaves,
abandoned love
when it is night

7

dogheaded
gods
who rise between

a cloud of butterflies,
the colors of the butterflies
illuminating

heads & eyes

when it is night

& we no longer

see

DREAMWORK ONE

for Barbara Einzig

to dream that he is walking past a window
to dream that the window moves & that the air around it turns
  to stone
to dream that he is being hit by stones
to dream of a window that reflects a stone
to dream that he is falling through a hole inside a stone
to dream of stones & boxes
to dream of standing on a black box like a coffin
to dream that he is dreaming of a stone
to dream of windows cracking in the street around him
to dream of wires tied around a stone
to dream of men with wires in their hands under his windows
to dream of hands that close over his eyes
& of other hands that close over his hands & belly
to dream of being in a country where the war has raged for
  years
to dream of flags & balconies
to dream of standing at a window watching the men in helmets
  stalking through his house
to dream of standing in his house & looking through a window
  watching the men in helmets on his street
to dream of men in helmets waiting at his door
to dream that his door is made of stone
to dream that he is standing at his door & screaming
that the men with wires in their hands have heard him scream
that the men in helmets shout a name he doesn't understand
to dream that he forgets his own name
to dream that he will get a new name in his dream
to dream of dreaming his new name
to dream a second time of dreaming
to dream his name in syllables
beginning with a name outrageously
in syllables
to dream of syllables & colors

to say his name is white & green
to dream of where the white & green are
there is a white stone & a green one
but there is not a white stone in his house
only a white reflection
a white hole in a stone
a green impediment reflecting a white stone
dreaming that he holds a white stone
that he learns to dream about the white stone's name
to dream outrageously
he learns to dream outrageously of hands
to dream of white & green hands
of hands reflecting colors from a stone
to dream of standing in a circle in a building in a dream
to dream that there are people with him in the circle
to dream that these are people he doesn't know
to dream that they are speaking a language he doesn't know
to dream that they don't know his language
to dream an alphabet in which to write his language
to change his alphabet from day to day
to dream an alphabet maybe a calendar for dreaming
to dream that he keeps the calendar inside his mouth
to dream on sunday that his mouth fills up with calendars
to dream on monday that a hand covers his mouth
to dream on tuesday that a bride sleeps in the hand
to dream on wednesday that the hand has grown a hundred
     nipples
to dream of hands & calendars on thursday
to dream on friday that a hand has lost its skin that his name
     has lost its syllables
to dream of emptiness on saturday
to dream that he is standing on an empty box that he is ham-
     mering against its sides
to dream that he is hammering a silence
to dream that the silence opens like an egg
to dream that the inside of the egg is labrador
a person in his dream says "labrador"
a person in his dream says "chalk"

to dream that a person in his dream says "solitaire"
to dream of walking with a person in his dream
to dream a face to dream that the face is on a person
to dream that the face is on a wall
to dream a face in stone
to dream a stone face deep inside a mirror
to dream that he had dreamed the face before
to dream that he was a child & dreaming of a face
the face is blue & lined with stripes
the face is like a mandrill's face a blue & red face
to dream that the face's stripes have faded
to dream that the face has lost its stripes that his name has
     lost its syllables
to dream a language without syllables
to dream that he understands this language
to dream that all of language is a single word
to dream that he knows this word
to dream that he forgets it
to dream that he explains the absence of this word
to dream that no one in the circle understands him
that he screams at them that he tells them that they're dream-
     ing
to dream that he has always dreamed
to dream that he has never woken up from dreaming

DREAMWORK TWO

the rabbi whispers to the rabbi:
little brother, you are gone
& never had existed

where is your sleep?
the rabbi calls out
where are your canticles?

he is no rabbi anyway
an indian he is
in jodhpurs & a cockeyed mask

the roar of treatises is silent now
the uncle dreams of newspapers
under the rabbi's hat

DREAMWORK THREE

a trembling old man dreams of a chinese garden
a comical old man dreams of newspapers under his rabbi's hat

.

a simple tavernkeeper dreams of icicles & fisheyes
a sinister tavernkeeper dreams of puddles with an angel of the
    law in every drop

.

the furrier's plump daughter is dreaming of a patch of old
    vanilla
the furrier's foreign daughter is dreaming of a hat from which
    a marten hangs

.

the proud accountant dreams of a trolleycar over the frozen
    river
the reluctant accountant dreams of his feet asleep in a fresh
    pair of red socks

.

the silly uncle dreams of a history written by a team of spanish
    doctors
the uncle in the next apartment dreams of the cost of katmandu

.

the retired gangster dreams of a right turn into a field of sacred
    lemons
the dancing gangster dreams of a carriage, a donkey, & a hand
    that holds the ace of spades

65

·

the grim man with a proposition dreams of his fingers entering
    a pair of gloves
the excited man with a proposition dreams of the letter E torn
    from the title of his poem

·

the remarkable elevator operator dreams of the marriage of
    karl marx
the easy elevator operator dreams of a seashell at the entry to
    the thirteenth floor

·

the candid photographer dreams of a wooden synagogue inside
    his brother's camera
the secret photographer dreams of a school of golden herrings
    drifting out to sea

·

the yiddish dadaist dreams of rare steaks & platonic pleasures
the rosy dadaist dreams that a honeycomb is being squashed
    against his face

·

the mysterious stranger dreams of a white tablecloth on which
    black threads are falling
the stranger whom no one sees dreams of his sister holding up
    a string of pearls

·

the asthmatic tax collector dreams of a row of sacred numbers
the rebellious tax collector dreams of a bathhouse set among
    old trees

•

the robust timber merchant dreams of a wind that blows inside
the blacksmith's bellows
the sobbing timber merchant dreams that his hands have
pressed the buttocks of his dreaming bride

•

the man with a fish between his teeth dreams of a famine for
forty-five days
the man dressed in white dreams of a potato

•

the savage gentile dreams of a dancer with flashy lightbulbs on
her shoes
the repentant gentile dreams of her fingers bringing honey to
his lips

•

the fancy barber dreams that his hands massage the captain's
neck
the silent barber dreams of a rooster with a thread tied to one
leg

•

the salty bridegroom dreams of horses galloping they swirl
around the bridegroom's house
the genuflecting bridegroom dreams of what his bride slides
through her fingers he sees it white & trembling in the
early sabbath light

•

the fat man in the derby dreams that it is spring that his seed
soon will be falling through an empty sky
the ecstatic man in the derby dreams that if he dreams it his
words will turn to flowers

DREAMWORK FOUR

"I have come back" he said
& stood outside her door
& pointed

he was his father, brightly wise

he was a ghost

he was his father's shadow on her lips

inside his mind a lake swam
& a moon swam in the lake

"defer it" said the man
& moved inside her

"it has all gathered in my mind"

"it will return"

1

in a corner of the old
synagogue, rosy
& blinking, the little
jews sit

peppers on their eyelids
form a tear
lacking a name, a drop
as black as sundays

when the dead have gone
the gardeners
will come in squads, the little
jews will watch them

entering the parks
at night, administering
the lives of
absent flowers

2

a toothless jew
in paradise   how gently

blow these winds
over miami

how sad the sinews
of leviathan, uncut

evenings in summer filled
with toothless jews

DREAMWORK SIX

1

ready yourself for death
the little woman
told me   hands on mine,
in portions, she had waited
half the night
unmoved, a victim
of how we couldn't speak
her name but always
stammering, objective
we held on by a thread
& started counting:
seven was her final word
before it broke in half

2

I feel my skin rip off
slowly
from its thin covering
& float over the sea:
my tongue cries out
my hands plunge down my sides
in jerky motion:
life becomes a comedy
like death
the audience of firemen
applauds
my skin goes searching
for another shore

DREAMWORK SEVEN   "The Belly"

the belly in the dream is central
to its mystery   the hairs
spread slowly toward the belly

& start the dreams again
in being there   a dream of penetrations
followed by a dream of bellies

a dream of rubber
bands   a belly
rubbed against its sheets

in jelly motions
or in a yellow dream
a dream of calendars in yellow

patient & dark dreams
a message that our lives move further
toward the dream time

bellied
bellying
belied

the tongue swells up with hunger
like a belly gliding upward
in a dream

SHAMAN DREAMWORK ONE

They cut his arm off & they laughed & he laughed back
They cut his other arm off & they laughed & he laughed back
They cut his leg off from the thigh & laughed & he laughed
    back
They cut his other leg off & they laughed & he laughed back
They cut his head off & they laughed & then his head laughed
    back

SHAMAN DREAMWORK TWO

I was moving through the water—somewhere in the middle of the ocean, someone said. I knew that I was sick & that the sickness meant my name would change. "Your name will be Diver," said the sickness, kicking up the water. That brought me to a mountain, which I climbed & found a naked woman waiting for me. I started sucking at her heart.

SHAMAN DREAMWORK THREE

quartz fragments
bore a hole in his tongue
& lodge there
hit him on his chest, his head
& the old man cuts out all his insides
empty, open to the glass
& rain
that floods him
"I am a lost man"
says the man
"the blacksmith made me
"dredged my floating bones up
"covered them with flesh
"there are, he said, three bones too many   weave a costume
"for each bone   he said   he forged a head for me   with
"letters on the inside I would learn to read   my eyes were
"changed to water & my ears   were punctured   so I could
"understand the language   flowers speak   I spoke with ma-
"rigolds   I spoke with gentians   cyclamens grew in my
"hair   my arms were empty stalks

SHAMAN DREAMWORK FOUR

his road went to the south,
red sand first,
then yellow gulleys,
then a magpie in the sky,
a crow behind it   song
releases you, the iron mountain
beckons, makes you
draw in your breath & fall
into a world of bones
a hole at center
you can plunge through

DREAM ANTHEMS

1

the patriots' dreams, the many
fruited flags & whispers
fish with the eyes of veterans that swim
under the ramparts
that swirl around the corners of the house
like flags   houses of flags
flags hung in amber
waving from chandeliers at sunset
spacious beds with flags
with purple sleepers wrapped in flags
& dreaming   flags in dreams
a galaxy of flags
fish flags illuminated
flags   fish stars exploding
old flags as good as gold
old promises
repeated by the senator the judge
stripped to his socks
& fiddling
eager to show his stripes
again
no eye without a tear
tonight in texas
watching the flags pass by

2

the dancing babe
removes a flag from
pubis   see the hairs
turn red
the blood turn into cream
blue shadows

in the dreams of
patriots
cover her pubis
as she walks

3

o banner so broad advancing
o ever-enlarging stars   (w. w.)

A THRENODY

the little jews are gone
their sacks are waiting for them
as once their mothers waited
at the embankment
watching the flags pass by

"it is time to buy a sherbet
"to pull a coin
"—a shekel—
"from your glove
"& pay the guard

he is a man made out of air
like you   a gypsy
or the brother of a gypsy
he will permit you to escape
the final toll

SEVEN FLAG POEMS

La Primavera

salute, compadres,
the flag of the great
      mother of us all
the goddess of america
raised high
salute her puffy
& parched cheeks, her banners,
nipples on the rise,
the ever benign crocuses that mark
the triumph of spring
in the beauty of the word *primavera,*
the day is terminal,
the goddess appearing for the party
stumbles & retreats,
she sends a spray into the air
& lets it fall,
sad & dependable,
the civic band
strikes up
the stars & stripes
forever

Flag Poem One

sad flag   fat girl
straddles a pump
her knees under her breasts
into each life a little
solitude   the juice
of energies seeps through
"make love beneath it"
sighs my heart
the red eye of her vulva
staring back

Flag Poem Two

the mystery behind
the weave   a star in place
right where the eye should be
blazons the prayer
the patriot wears over his heart
& shows the world
america in moonlight
tiny dervishes
how sticky are their tongues
tonight   how bright
their spangles

Flag Poem Three

the barber is a proud man

in his hand
a flag moves, driven
by the wind

the children of the lower states
cry out

o patriots' dreams
o alabaster cities

Flag Poem Four

over the city sleeps
the goddess
over the goddess
sleep the stars
& stripes
the universal flag
flaps on, the monstrous voice
resumes old energies
trapped in the cosmic wind

Flag Poem Five

flag mother sits
atop the hill
her cigar is a wandering star
her breasts balloons
with wavy stripes
up her abutments
red & white
they cover her body in the sky
like blood & milk
a baby patriot
plops from her womb

Flag Poem Six

"release the flag"
they tell him
"no" he roars   retreating
to the farmhouse
framed
he holds the varmints off
his fickle eye against the siding
"I repeat my stance
"I howl for ye
"proud little sisters, little stars
the evening slinks away
the cowboy stands
kneedeep in banners

Flag Poem Seven

the time called
hour of the flag
has struck   how bright
& fortunate
the crowd now can advance
with shiny shoes
their eyes
eager
like the eyes of children
or like the eyes of dogs
they are a faithful crowd
& each one
waves its tiny flag
the sign of their admission
to this crowd

RED BANNER FLAG POEM

trotsky's blood
is falling
it flows like banners down the stairs
& calls
the grandmothers from sleep
the generals surround
the bronx & carry him
dreaming to russia   brave
lev davidovich
the leader of the guard
on horseback   following
a flag

MILLENNIUM

Extremely beautiful, he makes a season out of lamb bones.

•

Never done vibrating.

•

A babe's head,
the fingers of a doll in empty space—
where is the tongue?
where are her sprockets?

•

The stove caught fire & a sewage pipe popped open. Outside,
they saw a car crushed by a brick wall.

•

The art of glossolalia, told with great serenity.

•

"I concede the first page to disaster. If you walk first, I walk
into a high room lined with flags. String out the messengers,
the representatives of vital interests, the privileged few. Glass
cuts through a bird in flight. The speed of silhouettes."

•

The remarkable collapse of history in history: the push toward
what we do not know, regretting & forgetting.

A drop of blood
below his navel.

.

"Between dreams, I felt the bed move. The walls cracked. I
saw a flash. Then my pelvis was pinned to the floor."

.

Cerulean.
Sunny.
Dappled with the orbs of night.

.

The lady said the field swayed back & forth, the corn going
down to the ground on one side coming up & going down to the
ground on the other.

.

Delicate cluster.
Flag of death.

.

Part of a mountain fell off & slid down over several farmers
in their houses just as they were waking.

.

Knock on wood.

.

On this night he was completely relaxed & was quietly praying
& praising God in English when suddenly he realized he was not
speaking English anymore, but a language unknown to him.

•

Thánatosána.

•

Venetian blinds started slapping against the windows & the high-rise elevators were wobbling on their rails.

•

Around 9:40 P.M., a woman at the front of the church made a cry &, with lifted arms, began to careen backwards away from the platform, turn, then come forward again. With spine & arms thrown backwards, she vainly tried to keep her balance. Finally she fell to the floor on her back & began to cry out Dadadadadada . . . .

•

My sacred one.
My mother.

•

Gardens of flags.

•

"They are buried in individual shrouds hurriedly prepared, & the ceremony doesn't last more than ten minutes . . . without a funeral prayer, without flowers."

•

The men ride on the men
like horses.
Silvery beauty—
ah my wooly white & crimson.

90

·

He shall be my amajuka.
He shall be my atandoboine.
He shall be my adala shilama pando baka shai bahikasai.
He shall be my adai.
He shall be my hekobai.
He shall be my blandahopendalabai.
He shall be my dahoken salabai.
He shall be my dasarabai.
He shall be my dahokentaia hokentai.
He shall be my dahokai.
He shall be my hokensala lipos salam.
He shall be my umbabadala shilama.

·

Poetry & truth
in conflict.
When the heart is full it flows out
through the mouth.

AMERICA A PROPHECY

"you'll be the first to be sacrificed"
the woman stops me on the street
to tell me
                    what does she mean?
how did she find me here to tell me?
was I waiting for her?
                            standing by our car,
the blue renault with sun roof,
in the early dusk,
somewhere in the shadow of the Pier Motel,
waiting for another car—a friend's—to round the corner,
lights on, & follow us
                    in sheol under
angel, curtain, covenant durations
                                    lately there have been many
such encounters   awake or dreaming
& I have begun to note them as they occur
& testify to prophecy
pathetic creams,
a drizzle of loose books
the prophet says
it is summer, it is the season of flags
the flags ignite over america
they light the sky over a sleeping world
the bodies of the sleepers
wrapped in the death the prophets
know is coming
waving their flags for death
fragments of holiness
the banner of a sad lost rite
light bearers
wheels
words tumbling down from ant hills
the pink lips of mothers against their sleeping babes

slip open, still asleep
　　　　　the tender minds absorbing
　　　　　　　stars & stripes
the dormitory of the patriotic dead
the flag room
flashbulbs diamond-studded cats
the tinny goddesses in love with drains
move through a night of smells
& puckered fetuses
wipe caca from their fingers
to mask the sacrifice
in which the dream is named
processions of the dead with dream names
walking, waking, waiting in the storm
the sacrifice has been afoot
for centuries　　　the murdered
sleepers, vagrant
under flags
striped bodies
heaving in great waves of sleepers
in the poisoned air
the votaries of spirit
ash, alhambra, albatross, departures
the sleepers grasp with spiny fingers
that even the dead can't dream away

THE NATURE THEATER OF OKLAHOMA (1)

someone arrives from tishimingo

it is practically Florida

it is practically the calories of summer

plin plin is the name for tea
in oklahoma

its curtains rise & fall

the shadow of a mirror
in a yellow lake

the shadow of a town called shootout

it is practically the way we are

it is practically the way the car toots
down the draw,
the car toots down the draw

THE NATURE THEATER OF OKLAHOMA (2)

the memory of god
is god   the cauliflower glistens
like a handkerchief
torn from the sun
& flailing   ice
& oranges
that conjure up her image
dimly
step into the light,
pale sister,
let the flies walk up your arm
in search of honey,
evading the tiny hairs,
their world
the mirror of your blue milk,
daughter of the sun,
the buds are red for you in oklahoma,
the birds are blue

THE NATURE THEATER OF OKLAHOMA (3)

pawnee bill rides bareback
into my smeared horizon

myths of soft eels

undulant
ambitious

they knock us off our feet

a black man
with his fist shoved up
a cow's ass

what a fancy smile!

what perfect choppers!

like the hands of god
in oklahoma

THE NATURE THEATER OF OKLAHOMA (4)

like the hands of god
in oklahoma
angels pray for you

the choirs wear
white robes   the dancers
prance in   leather
setting the final derrick up

the road to cowboy country,
scarcely a league away,
strides covered by a giant's gumshoes,
plumb forgotten,
oily

the land returns to
verdure   & the country
turns around
& names itself

OMEGA

THE NATURE THEATER OF OKLAHOMA (5)

"as simple as a dollar bill
"in oklahoma

the ides of march in shawnee

in the middle of a prairie
birds go nuts

they make a fallacy of fables

cadaverous
discolored

the fist sinks into its second face
the one seen in the corner
of the bar, the golden tooth
reflected in the mirror

a state of grace, a place
called oklahoma

THE NATURE THEATER OF OKLAHOMA (6)

"you are a bear" she said
& he became
a bear, he wore it
like his skin
the lost look
the interior grace
that surfaced on him,
he was faceless too
& walked inside
his footsteps   half
an animal who loves
his other half,
the silence of the moon
over his head,
this is the mark the man's arm
scribbles, darkly,
on the cave wall,
in the cave,
in oklahoma

the nature theater of oklahoma
opens   its little flags
flap recklessly
against the southern wind

a history of poetry
a history of jesus christ
a history of tishimingo

the cowhand plays
at coon can, holds
the final heart

the horse called kafka
cannot prance or turn

"I love your boots" she says

a history of where we are

THE NATURE THEATER OF OKLAHOMA (8)

in the heart of the indian territory of oklahoma

a chicken in every coop
a jesus in every garage

a tiger on every bush

the state of nature
in the state of oklahoma

old men & febrile women
in white shawls
that the grandfathers stitch with hexagrams

of a star as black as tar

o my oklahoma jesus

VISIONS OF JESUS

Let's say it was Jesus. Who is Jesus? Why should Jesus be the
    name
now celebrated, entering the poem?
Or let's say it wasn't. That I have the key to make it open
like a sound. Each sound's a rage.
Each page a turning over. I am writing this
the way a preacher speaks the word out on a prairie.
Visions of Jesus everywhere.
Sweet Jesus, says the song, to which the mind says
archly, darkly, "sour Jesus,"
& the poem begins with that.
Pink Jesus. Tiny Jesuses
on every bush, the world of sagebrush now a world of tiny
    Jesuses.
Soft Jesus maybe. (Is there a sexual aspersion in it
or only another way of saying "tender Jesus"?)
Jesus in Oklahoma
with his beard cut off. A weepy girl
named Jesus. She opens up her breast,
the moon pops out. O menses, colored glass
& papers, birds with messages
of love, tra la, on metal wings. His other name
is Rollo, Baby Winchester
or Baby Love. Jesus with a cow's head
on his shoulders, candles reaching from
his fingertips. Jesus in his one-eyed ford.
Squawk squawk, the preacher cries.
Eyes of the congregation turning white. The pinwheel
shooting sparks against his lap.
Jesus in furs. Jesus in Oklahoma,
growing old.
Hot & glowing Jesus. Jesus on the ace of hearts.
Alfalfa Jesus.
I am writing this the way a gambler cuts his name
into the table. Jesus in formica.

Drinking in the morning, playing coon-can
with his brother James.
Other names of Jesus.
Jesus H. Jones or Jesus in the woodpile.
Tomtom Jesus.
Jesus who aims a bullet down his mouth.
His children hang his body from a cross.
Three Jesuses in Ypsilanti.
Three in Tishimingo.
Jesus buried in Fort Sill.
His suffering has left their bodies
empty. In the night sky past El Reno
Jesus becomes his pain & flies,
aiming to leave his eyes for others.
Mother Jesus.
Her children have forsaken her.
She learns to cry & plays
nightly at mah jong, dropping her tiles
into the bottomless lake.
The man who chews his wrists down to the bone
is also Jesus. Jesus
in a feathered skull cap. Tacking stars
onto his vest, o cockeyed Jesus,
wanderer from Minsk,
he squawks the language of the little merchants,
squatting at their campfire he stirs
their coffee with *his* tool. How like his grandfather
he has become. Coyote Jesus.
Farting in the sweat lodge, tight
against his buttons
in the bride's room. Ponca City
Jesus. Pawnee Jesus.
He is staring at the eyes of Jesus
staring into his.
Their eyeballs spin around
like planets.
Visions of Jesus everywhere.
Gambler Jesus.

Banker Jesus.
Flatfoot Jesus with a floy floy.
Jesus shuffling.
The soldiers guard his silent fan,
tacked up, beside his rattle.
Jesus on the pavement. Jesus
shot for love, the powpow over,
naked, crawling toward you,
vomit on his beard. His father's milk
is dribbling—plin plin—in the cup
called Jesus. Ghosts
unhook the breast plate, draw
two streams of milk out,
mix them, opening
the mother's womb. No midwife
comes to her, she gives birth
like a man, & holds him
in a dream. Old song
erupting in the gourd dance,
in the storefront church
at night, among the hapless
armies. Two plus two is
Jesus. Five is Jesus.
Jesus in Okarchie,
driving. Jesus in his one-eyed ford,
arriving for the dance in Barefoot.
Visions of Jesus everywhere.
Jesus wrapped up in a woman's shawl.
Jesus in a corner,
stroking his tight body.
Masturbating Jesus.
Jesus sucking on a ball of fat.
There is no language left for him to speak,
only the humming in his chest,
a rush of syllables
like honey. Pouring
from every orifice, the voice
of renegades & preachers

without words.
Pink Jesuses in Oklahoma,
emerging with the spring.
Catfish Jesuses.
A beetle with the face of Jesus
scribbled on its back, squashed flat
against the dance floor.
Jesus squawking with the voice of angels.
I am writing this the way a man speaks without words.
Wordless in the light he pulls
out of his mouth. In the holes he hides in.
Wordless in praises. Wordless in peyote.
Wordless in hellos & hallelujahs.
The freaky Jew slips in beside
his bride, asleep forever, counts up bears
& cadillacs
under a leaky sky.

Oklahoma / 1985

A FLOWER CANTATA

1

he weaves his flowers into flower words,
a flower song beginning
that will become a flower word song
or will become a root song,
song root flowers at his beckoning
inside a house of flowers,
a flower world,
plumed flowers adrift
on flower drums
the fathers would call delicious flowers

2

she who would walk with pleasure flowers
would shake a flower rattle
in a house where flower copal burned,
where there was flower mist below the gates,
where flower rain fell down,
the sound of flower water
circled among the water flowers,
silent flowers,
beside the serpent flowers,
someone announced a paradise of flowers

3

here is a flower brilliance,
here where the mind forms turquoise flowers,
binds them in flower garlands,
turquoise swanlike flowers,
here where the bellbird flowers cry,
where the parrot flowers light a way for you,
here is a road of pink swan flowers,

a road of green swan water flowers,
the ruined flowers you walk among
in dreams, the lines of dead dry flowers

4

weeping flower tears they hide behind
sad flowers
that are weeping, weeping flowers
they would call flowers of bereavement
in the night, the drizzling flowers
are overwhelmed by flower sighs,
sad flower jewels stuck under their skins,
before the golden flowers have come to life
& hummed like darkness flowers,
the metal warriors of flower death

5

war flowers that draw us into war
awaken the knife death flowers for us
before the flower war deaths start,
we wait here among honeyed flowers
the drunken flowers that surround our hearts
like holy flowers
or the green swan cacao flowers of the fathers,
are there raven flowers there or flower ravens?
eagle & jaguar flowers?
or are there flower eagles, flower jaguars, flower ravens,
    chrome black ice blue flame red flowers?

6

sulfur flowers that turn into eagle flowers
or white lead flowers that turn into chalk & feather flowers
flower banners hanging in a field of sapphire flowers
or flower paintings buzzing like electric flowers

or like knifelike yellow flowers that turn into lightning
    flowers
while the fathers blow flower conch horns that explode like
    sonic flowers
or flower water conch horns that turn into siren flowers
in the sleep of yellow flowers urgent & muted like narcotic
    flowers
flower floods under a bridge of angel flowers
or plume flood flowers that turn into moon & planet flowers

7

my eye watches a world of flower fish
in which fish flowers shimmer,
laughing flowers in water kingdoms,
swimming toward flower pleasures,
these turn into flowers of the sun,
the true creation flowers
that are feather flowers in the daylight,
spirit flowers when the moon comes out
& turns them into flower ghosts
the fathers would call immortal feather flowers

A FLOWER CANTATA
"Coda & Variations"

shekinah incarnate in a flower fish
makes kingship flowers out of fish flowers,
where the hasidic flowers turn into laughing flowers,
messiah flowers throbbing with flower pleasures
watching—like flowers of the sun—the flower candles burn,
the alphabets with flower names light up: roses, thistles, true
    creation flowers, garlic, camomile, wood lilies, lemons,
    muscatel grapes, almonds, oranges, two apples, daisies,
    buckwheat, saffron, ice plants, figs, straw, wild tea, cherry,
    myrtle, a fruitful bough, the flowers of the priesthood
the feather flowers worn by women, menstrual flowers out of
    cracow, cracow flowers
on flowered streets, cracked boulevards where flower brides
    walk, spirit flowers
the flower ghosts will plant in holes the fathers sleep in,
immortal feather flowers on a map of flowers

Sources for most of the flower permutations, etc., are John Bierhorst's translation of the Aztec *Cantares Mexicanos* and J.R.'s *Poland/1931*.

A GLOSSARY FOR *KHURBN* & *OTHER POEMS*

In the poems contained herein—as with other poetry written head-on—there are some matters perfectly clear to me as author or transmitter of the work, that may be much less available to those reading it. Some of the circumstances of the title series are commented upon in the opening prose note to that series; specific words in other languages are sometimes translated in the text itself. The glossary below contains a few other such matters—by no means all—which I hope will be useful without compromising the sources from which the poems come. In the case of untranslated Yiddish words in particular, I would strongly urge the reader to catch them in their initial incomprehensibility before checking these notes towards their apparent "clarification."

The spellings of Polish place names, etc., have sometimes been modified toward something like their sounds in Yiddish.

Brunner: Alois Brunner, deputy and chief aide to Adolf Eichmann. Quoted 1987 in Chicago *Sun-Times:* "All of them deserved to die because they were the devil's agents and human *garbage. . . .* I have no regrets and would do it again."

Chelmno: concentration camp in Poland, to which children from Lidice (Czechoslovakia) were taken & murdered following the assassination, May 1942, of Gestapo chief Reinhard Heydrich, German Protector of Bohemia and Moravia.

[*dayn mamas bruder,* etc., pages 34–35]: your mother's brother vanished in the khurbn and must speak in my own tongue let me speak it through you the word khurbn // my eyes are blind from my khurbn I am now a corpse.

Dibbukim (Dibbiks): Spirits of those who die before their time & enter into (i.e. possess) the bodies of the living.

Elul: 12th month of the traditional Jewish (lunar) calendar, roughly equivalent to August–September.

[Erd, zolst nit, etc., page 11]: Earth, mayest thou not cover up my blood, and may there be no place left for my scream.

Gematria: a form of traditional Jewish numerology, playing off the fact that every letter of the Hebrew alphabet was also a number. Words & phrases whose letters added up to the same sum were intrinsically related. I have taken this as a means of composition, linking words/ideas by their numerical values in Hebrew. (See J.R., *The Gematria,* Sun & Moon Press.)

Gilgul: the one possessed, as by a dibbik.

Golem: A humanoid creature fashioned by magic, etc. Identified in its best known form with Rabbi Judah Loew ben Bezalel (1520–1609), whose thronelike chair still stands in the Oldnew Synagogue in Prague.

Hijikata: Tatsumi Hijikata, Japanese dancer/choreographer/writer, founder, post-Hiroshima, of expressionistic-traditional Butoh dance.

Ikon (1 and 2): An image from Austrian *volkskunde* museums of a fullbreasted woman dressed in a *dirndl,* with the bearded face of Jesus—& hanging from a cross. The story, as they tell it: that she was the *heilige kümmernis* (holy/saint misery), who, to avoid marriage, prayed for & received a beard, for which her father locked her in a tower, nailed christlike to a cross. Her release by a wandering minstrel (& her subsequent rescue of him when accused of her murder) didn't lead to marriage either but to a life apart. The image remains that of a female Jesus in extremis.

Khurbn (Yiddish, from Hebrew *khurban*): destruction, ruin, devastation, havoc, holocaust; used traditionally to describe the fate of the Jerusalem temple(s), thereafter for any widespread human disaster.

112

Lord of Caves: see J.R., *Technicians of the Sacred* (revised edition, University of California Press), page 318.

Malkin: Railtown near Treblinka, from which one went from Ostrov-Mazovietsk to, e.g., Warsaw.

Oswiecim (Polish), *Oshvie[n]tsim* (Yiddish): Auschwitz.

Ostrole[n]ka: town near Ostrov-Mazovietsk (Polish: Ostrow-Mazowiecka), birthplace (1900) of Esther (Lichtenstein) Rotenberg, from which her family fled to Ostrow-M. during the First World War.

Ruakh: spirit, animus; as, for example, the spirit (ruakh) of God upon the waters in Genesis 1.

Shadai: one of the names of God, sometimes translated as The Almighty; placed in amulets set into doorposts or worn about the neck.

Zohar: Book of Splendor; the central work of traditional Jewish mysticism, as kabbala.